50 Fairy-Tale Recipes

By: Kelly Johnson

Table of Contents

- Cinderella's Pumpkin Soup
- Sleeping Beauty's Rose Petal Jam
- Little Red Riding Hood's Berry Pie
- Snow White's Apple Dumplings
- Rapunzel's Golden Honey Bread
- Beauty and the Beast's Enchanted Rose Cake
- Peter Pan's Neverland Fruit Salad
- Jack and the Beanstalk's Bean Stew
- Goldilocks' Porridge with Honey
- The Frog Prince's Green Smoothie
- Alice in Wonderland's Mushroom Tart
- The Little Mermaid's Seaweed Salad
- Hansel and Gretel's Gingerbread Cookies
- The Snow Queen's Iced Lemon Cake
- Puss in Boots' Fancy Fish Pie
- Rumpelstiltskin's Spun Sugar Tarts
- The Nutcracker's Spiced Nuts

- The Ugly Duckling's Creamy Duck Breast
- The Princess and the Pea's Layered Cake
- Aladdin's Magic Carpet Flatbread
- Sleeping Beauty's Lavender Shortbread
- Cinderella's Midnight Cupcakes
- The Wizard of Oz's Rainbow Jello
- Pinocchio's Marzipan Mice
- The Twelve Dancing Princesses' Sparkling Punch
- The Little Red Hen's Wheat Bread
- The Elves and the Shoemaker's Chocolate Shoes
- Jack's Magic Beanstalk Soup
- Beauty and the Beast's Rose Petal Sorbet
- Snow White's Poison Apple Smoothie
- Thumbelina's Miniature Fruit Tarts
- The Golden Goose's Lemon Pudding
- The Fisherman and His Wife's Seafood Stew
- The Boy Who Cried Wolf's Lamb Chops
- The Pied Piper's Caramelized Apple Treats
- The Little Match Girl's Hot Cocoa

- Cinderella's Carriage Cookies
- The Goose Girl's Wild Herb Salad
- The Red Shoes' Cherry Sorbet
- The Twelve Huntsmen's Venison Stew
- The Firebird's Citrus Glazed Chicken
- The Golden Horn's Pastry Puffs
- The Princess and the Frog's Frog Legs
- The White Snake's Minted Lamb
- The Magic Fish's Stuffed Shells
- The Sandman's Dreamy Vanilla Pudding
- The Goose Girl's Honey-Cinnamon Biscotti
- The Little Prince's Asteroid Cake
- The Sorcerer's Stone's Dark Chocolate Truffles
- The Snow White's Snowflake Sugar Cookies

Cinderella's Pumpkin Soup

Ingredients:

- 2 cups pumpkin puree
- 1 onion, chopped
- 2 cloves garlic, minced
- 4 cups vegetable broth
- 1/2 cup heavy cream
- 1 tsp ground nutmeg
- 1 tsp cinnamon
- Salt and pepper to taste
- Olive oil for sautéing

Instructions:

1. In a large pot, heat olive oil over medium heat. Add chopped onion and garlic and sauté until softened.
2. Stir in the pumpkin puree, vegetable broth, nutmeg, cinnamon, salt, and pepper. Bring to a simmer.
3. Cook for about 20 minutes, stirring occasionally.
4. Use an immersion blender to blend the soup until smooth (or carefully blend in batches in a regular blender).
5. Stir in the heavy cream, taste, and adjust seasoning if necessary.
6. Serve hot, garnished with a swirl of cream and fresh herbs.

Sleeping Beauty's Rose Petal Jam

Ingredients:

- 2 cups rose petals (organic, unsprayed)
- 2 cups water
- 1 1/2 cups sugar
- 1 tbsp lemon juice
- 1 tbsp pectin (optional, for thicker jam)

Instructions:

1. Wash the rose petals thoroughly.
2. In a saucepan, bring water and rose petals to a boil. Reduce the heat and simmer for 10 minutes.
3. Strain the liquid into a bowl, pressing the petals to extract all the flavor.
4. Return the liquid to the saucepan, stir in sugar, and bring to a boil again.
5. Add lemon juice and optional pectin. Simmer for another 15 minutes, or until the jam reaches your desired consistency.
6. Pour into sterilized jars and seal while still hot. Let cool before serving.

Little Red Riding Hood's Berry Pie

Ingredients:

- 2 cups mixed berries (strawberries, raspberries, blueberries, etc.)
- 1/2 cup sugar
- 1 tbsp lemon juice
- 2 tbsp cornstarch
- 1 tbsp butter
- 1 package pie crust (or homemade)
- 1 egg (for egg wash)

Instructions:

1. Preheat your oven to 375°F (190°C).
2. In a bowl, combine the berries, sugar, lemon juice, and cornstarch. Stir until the berries are coated.
3. Roll out the pie crust and place it into a pie dish. Pour the berry mixture into the crust and dot with butter.
4. Cover with the second pie crust, crimping the edges to seal. Cut slits in the top to allow steam to escape.
5. Brush the top crust with a beaten egg to give it a golden finish.
6. Bake for 40-45 minutes, or until the crust is golden and the filling is bubbling.
7. Let cool before serving.

Snow White's Apple Dumplings

Ingredients:

- 2 large apples, peeled, cored, and cut into wedges
- 1 sheet puff pastry
- 1/4 cup brown sugar
- 1 tsp cinnamon
- 1/4 cup butter, melted
- 1/2 cup vanilla ice cream (optional, for serving)

Instructions:

1. Preheat the oven to 375°F (190°C).
2. In a small bowl, mix the brown sugar and cinnamon.
3. Roll out the puff pastry and cut it into squares large enough to wrap around each apple wedge.
4. Place an apple wedge in the center of each pastry square and sprinkle with cinnamon-sugar. Drizzle with melted butter.
5. Fold the pastry around the apples, sealing the edges.
6. Place the dumplings on a baking sheet and bake for 25-30 minutes, or until golden brown.
7. Serve with a scoop of vanilla ice cream if desired.

Rapunzel's Golden Honey Bread

Ingredients:

- 2 cups all-purpose flour
- 1/2 cup honey
- 1/4 cup butter, melted
- 1/2 cup milk
- 1 egg
- 2 tsp baking powder
- 1/4 tsp salt

Instructions:

1. Preheat the oven to 350°F (175°C) and grease a loaf pan.
2. In a large bowl, combine the flour, baking powder, and salt.
3. In another bowl, whisk together the honey, melted butter, milk, and egg.
4. Add the wet ingredients to the dry ingredients and stir until just combined.
5. Pour the batter into the prepared loaf pan and bake for 40-45 minutes, or until a toothpick inserted into the center comes out clean.
6. Let cool before slicing and serving.

Beauty and the Beast's Enchanted Rose Cake

Ingredients:

- 1 box red velvet cake mix (or homemade red velvet cake)
- 1/2 cup butter, softened
- 2 cups powdered sugar
- 1 tsp vanilla extract
- 3-4 tbsp milk
- Red food coloring (optional)
- Fresh rose petals for garnish

Instructions:

1. Bake the red velvet cake according to the instructions on the box (or homemade recipe).
2. Let the cake cool completely, then slice it in half horizontally to make two layers.
3. For the frosting, beat the butter, powdered sugar, vanilla, and milk until smooth. Add food coloring if desired to match the rose color.
4. Frost the top of one cake layer, then place the second layer on top. Frost the top and sides of the entire cake.
5. Garnish with fresh rose petals.
6. Serve the cake and let the magic unfold!

Peter Pan's Neverland Fruit Salad

Ingredients:

- 1 cup pineapple chunks
- 1 cup mango cubes
- 1 cup strawberries, sliced
- 1 cup blueberries
- 1 kiwi, peeled and sliced
- 2 tbsp fresh mint leaves, chopped
- 1 tbsp honey
- Juice of 1 lime

Instructions:

1. In a large bowl, combine all the fruits and mint.
2. In a small bowl, whisk together the honey and lime juice.
3. Pour the honey-lime dressing over the fruit and toss gently to combine.
4. Chill in the refrigerator for at least 30 minutes before serving.

Jack and the Beanstalk's Bean Stew

Ingredients:

- 2 cups white beans (such as cannellini or navy beans), cooked
- 1 onion, chopped
- 2 cloves garlic, minced
- 3 carrots, diced
- 3 celery stalks, chopped
- 4 cups vegetable broth
- 1 tsp thyme
- Salt and pepper to taste
- Olive oil for sautéing

Instructions:

1. In a large pot, heat olive oil over medium heat. Sauté the onion, garlic, carrots, and celery until softened.
2. Add the cooked beans, vegetable broth, thyme, salt, and pepper.
3. Bring to a boil, then reduce the heat and simmer for 30 minutes to allow the flavors to meld.
4. Serve hot, garnished with fresh herbs.

Goldilocks' Porridge with Honey

Ingredients:

- 1 cup rolled oats
- 2 cups milk (or water)
- 2 tbsp honey
- 1/4 tsp cinnamon
- A pinch of salt
- Fresh berries or sliced bananas for topping

Instructions:

1. In a saucepan, bring the milk (or water) to a simmer.
2. Stir in the oats, honey, cinnamon, and salt.
3. Cook for 5-7 minutes, stirring occasionally, until the oats are soft and creamy.
4. Top with fresh berries or sliced bananas and serve warm.

The Frog Prince's Green Smoothie

Ingredients:

- 1 cup spinach
- 1/2 cup frozen mango
- 1/2 banana
- 1/2 cup coconut water (or water)
- 1 tbsp honey (optional)
- 1 tsp chia seeds (optional)

Instructions:

1. Place all ingredients into a blender.
2. Blend until smooth and creamy. Add more coconut water if you prefer a thinner consistency.
3. Pour into a glass and serve immediately for a healthy and magical green treat!

Alice in Wonderland's Mushroom Tart

Ingredients:

- 1 sheet puff pastry
- 1 cup mushrooms, sliced (button, cremini, or a mix)
- 1 small onion, finely chopped
- 1 tbsp butter
- 1/4 cup grated Gruyère or Swiss cheese
- 1/4 cup heavy cream
- Salt and pepper to taste
- Fresh thyme (optional)

Instructions:

1. Preheat the oven to 375°F (190°C). Roll out the puff pastry and place it in a tart pan or on a baking sheet.
2. Sauté the mushrooms and onion in butter until soft and browned, about 7-10 minutes.
3. In a bowl, mix the heavy cream, grated cheese, salt, and pepper. Stir in the sautéed mushrooms.
4. Pour the mixture into the prepared pastry shell.
5. Bake for 20-25 minutes, or until golden and crispy. Garnish with fresh thyme if desired.
6. Let cool slightly before slicing and serving.

The Little Mermaid's Seaweed Salad

Ingredients:

- 1 cup wakame seaweed (dried)
- 1 cucumber, thinly sliced
- 1 carrot, julienned
- 2 tbsp rice vinegar
- 1 tbsp soy sauce
- 1 tsp sesame oil
- 1 tsp honey
- Sesame seeds for garnish
- Fresh cilantro for garnish

Instructions:

1. Rehydrate the wakame seaweed by soaking it in warm water for 10-15 minutes, then drain and pat dry.
2. In a bowl, combine the seaweed, cucumber, and carrot.
3. In a small bowl, whisk together rice vinegar, soy sauce, sesame oil, and honey.
4. Pour the dressing over the salad and toss gently.
5. Garnish with sesame seeds and cilantro before serving.

Hansel and Gretel's Gingerbread Cookies

Ingredients:

- 2 1/4 cups all-purpose flour
- 1 tbsp ground ginger
- 1 tsp ground cinnamon
- 1/2 tsp ground cloves
- 1/2 tsp baking soda
- 1/2 cup unsalted butter, softened
- 1/2 cup brown sugar
- 1/2 cup molasses
- 1 large egg

Instructions:

1. Preheat the oven to 350°F (175°C). Line baking sheets with parchment paper.
2. In a bowl, whisk together flour, ginger, cinnamon, cloves, and baking soda.
3. In another bowl, cream together the butter, brown sugar, and molasses until smooth.
4. Add the egg and beat well. Gradually add the dry ingredients, mixing until a dough forms.
5. Roll out the dough on a floured surface and cut into gingerbread shapes with cookie cutters.

6. Bake for 8-10 minutes, or until firm. Let cool on a wire rack before decorating with icing or sprinkles.

The Snow Queen's Iced Lemon Cake

Ingredients:

- 1 1/2 cups all-purpose flour
- 1 cup sugar
- 1/2 cup unsalted butter, softened
- 2 large eggs
- 1/2 cup sour cream
- Zest and juice of 2 lemons
- 1 tsp vanilla extract
- 1 tsp baking powder
- Powdered sugar for dusting

Instructions:

1. Preheat the oven to 350°F (175°C). Grease and flour a 9-inch round cake pan.
2. In a bowl, whisk together the flour, baking powder, and a pinch of salt.
3. In another bowl, beat the butter and sugar until light and fluffy. Add the eggs one at a time, beating well after each addition.
4. Mix in the sour cream, lemon zest, lemon juice, and vanilla extract.
5. Gradually add the dry ingredients and stir until just combined.
6. Pour the batter into the prepared cake pan and bake for 25-30 minutes, or until a toothpick comes out clean.

7. Let the cake cool before dusting with powdered sugar for a snowy finish.

Puss in Boots' Fancy Fish Pie

Ingredients:

- 1 lb white fish fillets (such as cod or haddock)
- 1/2 cup peas
- 1 onion, chopped
- 2 tbsp butter
- 1/4 cup all-purpose flour
- 2 cups milk
- 1/2 cup grated cheddar cheese
- 2 tbsp fresh parsley, chopped
- 1 sheet puff pastry
- Salt and pepper to taste

Instructions:

1. Preheat the oven to 400°F (200°C).
2. Cook the fish fillets in a pan until flaky, then flake them into bite-sized pieces.
3. In another pan, melt the butter and sauté the onions until soft.
4. Stir in the flour and cook for 1-2 minutes. Gradually whisk in the milk, and cook until the sauce thickens.
5. Add the flaked fish, peas, cheese, parsley, salt, and pepper. Stir well to combine.

6. Pour the mixture into a pie dish and cover with puff pastry. Trim any excess pastry and press the edges to seal.

7. Bake for 25-30 minutes, or until the pastry is golden and puffed.

8. Serve hot, garnished with additional parsley.

Rumpelstiltskin's Spun Sugar Tarts

Ingredients:

- 1 sheet puff pastry
- 1/4 cup sugar (for spun sugar)
- 1/2 cup lemon curd
- Fresh berries for topping

Instructions:

1. Preheat the oven to 375°F (190°C). Roll out the puff pastry and cut into circles to fit mini tart pans.
2. Place the pastry into the tart pans and bake for 12-15 minutes, or until golden and puffed.
3. While the tarts are baking, melt the sugar in a small saucepan over medium heat until it turns golden.
4. To make spun sugar, pour the melted sugar onto a parchment paper-lined surface. Once cool, use a fork to spin the sugar into delicate threads.
5. Once the tarts are cooled, fill them with lemon curd and top with fresh berries and spun sugar.
6. Serve immediately, as the spun sugar will begin to dissolve over time.

The Nutcracker's Spiced Nuts

Ingredients:

- 1 cup mixed nuts (almonds, pecans, walnuts)
- 1 tbsp olive oil
- 1 tsp cinnamon
- 1/2 tsp ground ginger
- 1/2 tsp nutmeg
- 1/4 tsp cayenne pepper (optional)
- 1 tbsp honey
- Salt to taste

Instructions:

1. Preheat the oven to 350°F (175°C). Line a baking sheet with parchment paper.
2. Toss the mixed nuts in olive oil, cinnamon, ginger, nutmeg, cayenne (if using), honey, and a pinch of salt.
3. Spread the nuts in a single layer on the baking sheet and bake for 10-15 minutes, stirring once, until golden brown.
4. Let cool before serving.

The Ugly Duckling's Creamy Duck Breast

Ingredients:

- 2 duck breasts, skin on
- 1/2 cup heavy cream
- 1 tbsp Dijon mustard
- 1/2 cup chicken broth
- 1 tbsp olive oil
- Salt and pepper to taste
- Fresh thyme sprigs (optional)

Instructions:

1. Score the skin of the duck breasts and season with salt and pepper.
2. Heat olive oil in a pan over medium heat. Place the duck breasts skin-side down and cook for 5-7 minutes, rendering the fat and crisping the skin.
3. Flip the duck breasts and cook for an additional 4-5 minutes, or until the internal temperature reaches 135°F (57°C) for medium-rare.
4. Remove the duck breasts and let them rest.
5. In the same pan, add chicken broth and scrape up any browned bits. Stir in mustard and heavy cream, simmering until the sauce thickens, about 3-4 minutes.
6. Slice the duck and drizzle the creamy sauce over the top. Garnish with fresh thyme.

The Princess and the Pea's Layered Cake

Ingredients:

- 1 box vanilla cake mix (or your favorite homemade recipe)
- 1/4 cup raspberry jam
- 1/4 cup lemon curd
- 1 cup butter, softened
- 4 cups powdered sugar
- 1 tsp vanilla extract
- A few drops of pink food coloring (optional)

Instructions:

1. Preheat the oven according to the cake mix instructions and prepare the cake pans.
2. Bake the cakes according to the package instructions and allow them to cool completely.
3. Once the cakes have cooled, slice each cake horizontally into two layers.
4. Spread a layer of raspberry jam on the bottom layer, followed by lemon curd on the next layer, stacking the layers carefully.
5. For the frosting, beat the butter with powdered sugar and vanilla extract until light and fluffy. If you'd like, add a few drops of pink food coloring.
6. Frost the outside of the cake generously, making sure to cover all sides with the creamy frosting.
7. Decorate the top with fresh berries or edible flowers for a regal finish.

Aladdin's Magic Carpet Flatbread

Ingredients:

- 2 cups all-purpose flour
- 1 tsp salt
- 1 tsp baking powder
- 2 tbsp olive oil
- 3/4 cup water
- 1 tbsp sesame seeds (optional)
- Fresh parsley for garnish

Instructions:

1. In a bowl, mix flour, salt, and baking powder. Add olive oil and water, then stir to combine into a dough.
2. Knead the dough for 5-7 minutes until smooth and elastic. Let it rest for 30 minutes covered with a damp cloth.
3. Preheat a skillet over medium-high heat. Divide the dough into small balls and roll them out into flatbreads.
4. Cook each flatbread for about 2-3 minutes on each side until golden and puffed up.
5. Optional: Sprinkle with sesame seeds while cooking.
6. Garnish with chopped fresh parsley and serve warm.

Sleeping Beauty's Lavender Shortbread

Ingredients:

- 2 cups all-purpose flour
- 1/4 cup powdered sugar
- 1/2 tsp dried lavender
- 1 cup unsalted butter, softened
- 1 tsp vanilla extract
- 1/4 tsp salt

Instructions:

1. Preheat your oven to 325°F (163°C). Line a baking sheet with parchment paper.
2. In a bowl, beat the butter and powdered sugar together until smooth. Add vanilla extract and dried lavender.
3. Gradually add the flour and salt, mixing until a dough forms.
4. Roll out the dough to 1/4-inch thickness and cut into shapes (squares or circles).
5. Place the cookies on the baking sheet and bake for 10-12 minutes, or until lightly golden at the edges.
6. Let cool on a wire rack before serving.

Cinderella's Midnight Cupcakes

Ingredients:

- 1 box of vanilla cake mix (or your favorite homemade recipe)
- 1 cup heavy cream
- 1/4 cup powdered sugar
- 1 tsp vanilla extract
- Blue food coloring (optional)
- Edible glitter (optional)

Instructions:

1. Prepare the cupcakes according to the package instructions or your recipe, and bake them in lined cupcake tins.

2. While the cupcakes cool, whip the heavy cream with powdered sugar and vanilla extract until stiff peaks form. If you'd like, add a drop of blue food coloring to create a magical midnight blue frosting.

3. Frost the cooled cupcakes with the whipped cream mixture and top with edible glitter for extra sparkle.

4. Serve these magical treats at your next enchanted gathering!

The Wizard of Oz's Rainbow Jello

Ingredients:

- 6 different colors of Jello (e.g., red, orange, yellow, green, blue, purple)
- 2 cups boiling water (for each color)
- 1 cup cold water (for each color)
- 1 cup sweetened condensed milk (optional, for creamy layers)

Instructions:

1. Prepare each color of Jello separately by dissolving the gelatin in boiling water, then stirring in cold water.
2. Pour the first color of Jello into a clear glass dish and refrigerate until set, about 1 hour.
3. Once the first layer is set, mix a small amount of sweetened condensed milk into the next color of Jello, then pour it gently over the first layer. Refrigerate again until set.
4. Repeat this process with each color, layering the Jello and allowing each layer to set before adding the next.
5. Once all the layers are set, serve chilled for a rainbow of fun and flavor.

Pinocchio's Marzipan Mice

Ingredients:

- 1 cup marzipan
- 1/4 cup powdered sugar
- 2 small chocolate chips (for eyes)
- 1 almond (for ears)
- 1 pink candy (for nose)

Instructions:

1. Roll small pieces of marzipan into oval shapes to form the body of the mice.
2. Shape a small piece of marzipan into a tail and attach it to the body.
3. Use chocolate chips as eyes and a pink candy (like a jellybean or small gumball) for the nose.
4. Slice almonds into thin pieces and place them on the sides of the marzipan mice as ears.
5. Serve as cute edible treats at your next fairy tale-themed party.

The Twelve Dancing Princesses' Sparkling Punch

Ingredients:

- 4 cups sparkling water or lemon-lime soda
- 1 cup orange juice
- 1/2 cup pineapple juice
- 1/4 cup grenadine syrup
- Fresh fruit slices (oranges, lemons, berries) for garnish

Instructions:

1. In a large pitcher, combine the sparkling water (or soda), orange juice, and pineapple juice.
2. Add grenadine syrup and stir gently to mix.
3. Add fresh fruit slices for an extra colorful and refreshing touch.
4. Serve chilled, and enjoy this bubbly and sparkling fairy tale-inspired drink.

The Little Red Hen's Wheat Bread

Ingredients:

- 2 cups whole wheat flour
- 1 cup all-purpose flour
- 1 packet active dry yeast
- 1 tsp salt
- 1 tbsp sugar
- 1 tbsp olive oil
- 1 cup warm water

Instructions:

1. In a large bowl, combine the warm water, sugar, and yeast. Let sit for 5-10 minutes, until bubbly and frothy.
2. Add the whole wheat flour, all-purpose flour, and salt to the yeast mixture. Mix until a dough forms.
3. Knead the dough for 5-7 minutes until smooth. Place it in an oiled bowl, cover with a cloth, and let rise for about 1 hour, or until doubled in size.
4. Preheat the oven to 375°F (190°C).
5. Punch down the dough, shape it into a loaf, and place it on a greased baking pan.
6. Bake for 25-30 minutes, or until the bread sounds hollow when tapped on the bottom.
7. Let cool slightly before slicing and serving.

The Elves and the Shoemaker's Chocolate Shoes

Ingredients:

- 1 box chocolate cake mix (or your favorite homemade chocolate cake recipe)
- 1/2 cup butter, melted
- 1/4 cup milk
- 2 cups powdered sugar
- 1 tsp vanilla extract
- 2 tbsp cocoa powder
- Small candy shoes or shaped chocolate molds (optional)

Instructions:

1. Bake the chocolate cake according to the package instructions or your homemade recipe, then let it cool completely.
2. Once cooled, crumble the cake into small pieces.
3. In a mixing bowl, combine the crumbled cake with melted butter, milk, powdered sugar, and vanilla extract. Mix until the mixture holds together when pressed.
4. Shape the cake mixture into small "shoe" shapes. If using candy molds or shaped chocolate molds, press the mixture into the molds and chill for 30 minutes.
5. Once set, frost the chocolate shoes with cocoa frosting, and decorate with edible glitter or sprinkles to add a touch of magic.

Jack's Magic Beanstalk Soup

Ingredients:

- 1 cup green beans, chopped
- 1 cup peas
- 1 small onion, chopped
- 2 garlic cloves, minced
- 4 cups vegetable broth
- 1 tbsp olive oil
- Salt and pepper to taste
- 1 tbsp lemon juice
- Fresh parsley for garnish

Instructions:

1. Heat olive oil in a large pot over medium heat. Add the chopped onion and garlic, cooking until softened.
2. Add the green beans and peas, sautéing for a few minutes.
3. Pour in the vegetable broth, bring to a simmer, and cook for 10-15 minutes, until the vegetables are tender.
4. Season with salt, pepper, and lemon juice.
5. Use an immersion blender to blend the soup until smooth, or leave it chunky if preferred.
6. Garnish with fresh parsley and serve.

Beauty and the Beast's Rose Petal Sorbet

Ingredients:

- 1 cup fresh rose petals (organic, pesticide-free)
- 1 cup water
- 1/2 cup sugar
- 1/2 cup lemon juice
- 2 cups ice

Instructions:

1. Rinse the rose petals and remove any stems.
2. In a saucepan, combine the water and sugar. Heat until the sugar dissolves completely.
3. Add the rose petals to the syrup and simmer for about 5 minutes. Remove from heat and let steep for 15 minutes.
4. Strain the syrup to remove the petals and add the lemon juice.
5. Pour the syrup into a shallow dish, then place it in the freezer. After 30 minutes, use a fork to scrape the frozen syrup into ice crystals.
6. Continue to freeze and scrape every 30 minutes for about 3 hours until the sorbet reaches the desired texture.
7. Serve in chilled bowls, garnished with fresh rose petals.

Snow White's Poison Apple Smoothie

Ingredients:

- 1 apple, cored and sliced
- 1/2 banana
- 1/2 cup spinach
- 1/2 cup Greek yogurt
- 1/4 tsp cinnamon
- 1 tbsp honey (optional)
- 1/2 cup almond milk

Instructions:

1. In a blender, combine all the ingredients and blend until smooth.
2. Taste and adjust sweetness with honey if needed.
3. Pour into a glass and serve chilled for a refreshing yet "magical" treat!

Thumbelina's Miniature Fruit Tarts

Ingredients:

- 1 package mini tart shells (or homemade shortcrust pastry)
- 1/2 cup whipped cream cheese
- 1/4 cup powdered sugar
- 1/2 tsp vanilla extract
- Fresh berries (strawberries, blueberries, raspberries)
- Fresh mint for garnish

Instructions:

1. Preheat the oven and bake the mini tart shells according to package instructions.
2. In a mixing bowl, beat the cream cheese with powdered sugar and vanilla extract until smooth.
3. Once the tart shells are cooled, fill them with the cream cheese mixture.
4. Top each tart with a selection of fresh berries and garnish with mint leaves.
5. Serve as mini desserts for a delightful fairy-tale treat.

The Golden Goose's Lemon Pudding

Ingredients:

- 1/2 cup fresh lemon juice (about 2 lemons)
- 1 cup milk
- 3/4 cup sugar
- 2 tbsp cornstarch
- 1/4 tsp salt
- 2 large egg yolks
- 2 tbsp butter
- Lemon zest for garnish

Instructions:

1. In a saucepan, combine the sugar, cornstarch, and salt. Gradually whisk in the milk until smooth.

2. Heat over medium heat, stirring constantly until the mixture thickens, about 5 minutes.

3. In a separate bowl, whisk the egg yolks. Gradually add some of the hot milk mixture to the yolks to temper them, then slowly pour the egg mixture back into the saucepan, whisking constantly.

4. Continue cooking for another 2-3 minutes until thickened.

5. Stir in the lemon juice, butter, and lemon zest.

6. Pour into individual serving bowls and refrigerate for at least 2 hours before serving.

The Fisherman and His Wife's Seafood Stew

Ingredients:

- 1 lb shrimp, peeled and deveined
- 1/2 lb white fish fillets (cod, halibut, etc.)
- 1/2 lb mussels, cleaned
- 1 cup white wine
- 1 cup seafood stock
- 2 garlic cloves, minced
- 1 onion, chopped
- 2 tomatoes, chopped
- 1/4 cup fresh parsley, chopped
- 1 tbsp olive oil
- Salt and pepper to taste

Instructions:

1. Heat olive oil in a large pot over medium heat. Add the garlic and onion, cooking until softened.

2. Add the tomatoes, wine, and seafood stock to the pot, bringing it to a simmer.

3. Add the shrimp, fish fillets, and mussels to the pot. Cook for about 5-7 minutes, until the shrimp turn pink and the mussels open.

4. Season with salt and pepper, and stir in fresh parsley just before serving.

5. Serve the seafood stew with crusty bread on the side for a hearty meal.

The Boy Who Cried Wolf's Lamb Chops

Ingredients:

- 4 lamb chops
- 2 tbsp olive oil
- 2 garlic cloves, minced
- 1 tbsp fresh rosemary, chopped
- 1 tbsp fresh thyme, chopped
- Salt and pepper to taste
- 1 tbsp lemon zest

Instructions:

1. Preheat your grill or stovetop pan over medium-high heat.
2. Rub the lamb chops with olive oil, garlic, rosemary, thyme, salt, and pepper.
3. Grill or sear the lamb chops for 4-5 minutes on each side for medium-rare, or longer to your preferred doneness.
4. Garnish with lemon zest and serve with a side of mint jelly or roasted vegetables.

The Pied Piper's Caramelized Apple Treats

Ingredients:

- 4 apples, peeled and sliced
- 1/4 cup butter
- 1/4 cup brown sugar
- 1 tsp cinnamon
- 1/2 tsp nutmeg
- 1 tbsp lemon juice
- Chopped walnuts (optional)

Instructions:

1. In a large skillet, melt butter over medium heat.
2. Add the apple slices, brown sugar, cinnamon, and nutmeg. Cook, stirring occasionally, for 10-15 minutes until the apples are soft and caramelized.
3. Add the lemon juice and stir well.
4. Serve the caramelized apples warm, topped with chopped walnuts for extra crunch, if desired.

The Little Match Girl's Hot Cocoa

Ingredients:

- 2 cups milk (or dairy-free milk of choice)
- 1/4 cup cocoa powder
- 1/4 cup sugar
- 1 tsp vanilla extract
- 1 pinch of salt
- Whipped cream and chocolate shavings for topping

Instructions:

1. In a small saucepan, heat the milk over medium heat.
2. Whisk in the cocoa powder, sugar, vanilla extract, and salt until smooth.
3. Continue heating until the cocoa is hot but not boiling.
4. Pour into a mug and top with whipped cream and chocolate shavings.
5. Serve with a side of crispy cookies for a cozy treat.

Cinderella's Carriage Cookies

Ingredients:

- 1 cup unsalted butter, softened
- 1 cup powdered sugar
- 2 cups all-purpose flour
- 1/2 tsp vanilla extract
- Pinch of salt
- Edible gold dust for decoration

Instructions:

1. Preheat the oven to 350°F (175°C).
2. In a mixing bowl, cream together butter and powdered sugar until light and fluffy.
3. Add the vanilla extract, salt, and flour, mixing until just combined.
4. Roll the dough into 1-inch balls and place them on a baking sheet.
5. Flatten slightly with a fork or your hands, and bake for 10-12 minutes, or until the edges are golden.
6. Once cooled, sprinkle with edible gold dust to resemble Cinderella's magical carriage.

The Goose Girl's Wild Herb Salad

Ingredients:

- 2 cups mixed greens (arugula, spinach, kale, etc.)
- 1/4 cup fresh mint leaves, torn
- 1/4 cup fresh basil leaves, torn
- 1/4 cup parsley, chopped
- 1/4 cup goat cheese, crumbled
- 1/4 cup walnuts, toasted
- 2 tbsp olive oil
- 1 tbsp lemon juice
- Salt and pepper to taste

Instructions:

1. In a large bowl, toss the mixed greens with mint, basil, and parsley.
2. Add the goat cheese and toasted walnuts, mixing gently.
3. Drizzle with olive oil and lemon juice, and season with salt and pepper.
4. Serve immediately as a fresh and fragrant side salad.

The Red Shoes' Cherry Sorbet

Ingredients:

- 3 cups fresh cherries, pitted
- 1/2 cup sugar
- 1 tbsp lemon juice
- 1/2 cup water

Instructions:

1. In a blender, combine the cherries, sugar, lemon juice, and water. Blend until smooth.
2. Pour the mixture into a shallow dish or ice cream maker.
3. If using a shallow dish, place it in the freezer, scraping with a fork every 30 minutes until it reaches a sorbet-like texture, about 2-3 hours.
4. If using an ice cream maker, churn according to the manufacturer's instructions.
5. Serve in bowls and garnish with fresh cherries for a beautiful red hue.

The Twelve Huntsmen's Venison Stew

Ingredients:

- 1 lb venison stew meat
- 1 tbsp olive oil
- 1 onion, chopped
- 2 garlic cloves, minced
- 3 carrots, sliced
- 3 potatoes, diced
- 1 cup red wine
- 4 cups beef broth
- 2 tsp thyme
- 2 bay leaves
- Salt and pepper to taste

Instructions:

1. In a large pot, heat olive oil over medium heat. Brown the venison stew meat on all sides, then remove from the pot and set aside.

2. In the same pot, sauté the onion and garlic until softened.

3. Add the carrots, potatoes, red wine, beef broth, thyme, and bay leaves. Stir well.

4. Return the venison to the pot and bring to a simmer. Cover and cook for 2-3 hours, or until the meat is tender.

5. Season with salt and pepper, and serve hot.

The Firebird's Citrus Glazed Chicken

Ingredients:

- 4 chicken breasts
- 1/4 cup fresh orange juice
- 1/4 cup lemon juice
- 2 tbsp honey
- 1 tbsp soy sauce
- 1 garlic clove, minced
- Salt and pepper to taste

Instructions:

1. In a small bowl, whisk together the orange juice, lemon juice, honey, soy sauce, garlic, salt, and pepper.
2. Preheat your grill or stovetop pan over medium heat.
3. Brush the chicken breasts with the citrus glaze and cook for 5-7 minutes on each side, basting occasionally with the glaze, until the chicken is fully cooked.
4. Serve the chicken with a drizzle of the leftover glaze and garnish with citrus slices.

The Golden Horn's Pastry Puffs

Ingredients:

- 1 package puff pastry sheets
- 1/2 cup ricotta cheese
- 1/4 cup Parmesan cheese, grated
- 1 egg, beaten
- 1 tbsp fresh thyme, chopped
- 1/4 tsp salt
- 1/4 tsp black pepper

Instructions:

1. Preheat the oven to 400°F (200°C).
2. Roll out the puff pastry sheets and cut them into squares or triangles.
3. In a bowl, mix the ricotta, Parmesan, egg, thyme, salt, and pepper.
4. Spoon a small amount of the cheese mixture onto each pastry square and fold into triangles or corners, sealing the edges.
5. Place the pastry puffs on a baking sheet and brush with the beaten egg.
6. Bake for 15-20 minutes, or until golden and puffed up.
7. Serve warm as a savory treat.

The Princess and the Frog's Frog Legs

Ingredients:

- 12 frog legs
- 1/4 cup flour
- 1/4 tsp garlic powder
- 1/4 tsp cayenne pepper
- Salt and pepper to taste
- 1/2 cup butter
- 1 tbsp fresh parsley, chopped
- 1 tbsp lemon juice

Instructions:

1. Pat the frog legs dry and season with salt, pepper, garlic powder, and cayenne.
2. Dredge the frog legs in flour, shaking off excess.
3. In a skillet, melt the butter over medium heat. Add the frog legs and cook for about 3-4 minutes per side, until golden and cooked through.
4. Remove from heat, drizzle with lemon juice, and sprinkle with fresh parsley.
5. Serve immediately with a side of garlic butter for dipping.

The White Snake's Minted Lamb

Ingredients:

- 1 rack of lamb (8 ribs)
- 2 tbsp olive oil
- 2 tbsp fresh mint, chopped
- 1 tbsp rosemary, chopped
- 3 garlic cloves, minced
- Salt and pepper to taste
- 1/4 cup balsamic vinegar
- 1/4 cup honey

Instructions:

1. Preheat the oven to 400°F (200°C).
2. Rub the lamb rack with olive oil, mint, rosemary, garlic, salt, and pepper.
3. Roast the lamb for 20-25 minutes for medium-rare or longer for desired doneness.
4. In a small saucepan, combine balsamic vinegar and honey, simmering until thickened, about 5 minutes.
5. Once the lamb is done, let it rest for 5 minutes before slicing.
6. Drizzle the balsamic-honey glaze over the lamb and serve with a mint garnish.

The Magic Fish's Stuffed Shells

Ingredients:

- 12 large pasta shells
- 1 cup ricotta cheese
- 1/2 cup mozzarella cheese, shredded
- 1/4 cup Parmesan cheese, grated
- 1 egg
- 1 cup spinach, cooked and chopped
- 2 cups marinara sauce
- Fresh basil for garnish

Instructions:

1. Preheat the oven to 375°F (190°C). Cook the pasta shells according to package directions. Drain and set aside.

2. In a bowl, mix the ricotta, mozzarella, Parmesan, egg, spinach, salt, and pepper.

3. Stuff the cooked pasta shells with the cheese mixture.

4. Spread marinara sauce in the bottom of a baking dish. Place the stuffed shells on top, then pour the remaining marinara sauce over them.

5. Cover with foil and bake for 25 minutes. Remove foil and bake for another 5-10 minutes until bubbly.

6. Garnish with fresh basil and serve hot.

The Sandman's Dreamy Vanilla Pudding

Ingredients:

- 2 cups whole milk
- 1/2 cup sugar
- 2 large egg yolks
- 3 tbsp cornstarch
- 1 tbsp vanilla extract
- Pinch of salt
- Whipped cream for topping

Instructions:

1. In a saucepan, whisk together the milk, sugar, and egg yolks. Heat over medium heat, whisking constantly.
2. In a small bowl, dissolve cornstarch in a little milk and add to the saucepan. Continue whisking until the mixture thickens, about 5-7 minutes.
3. Remove from heat, stir in vanilla extract and a pinch of salt.
4. Pour the pudding into serving cups and let it cool to room temperature before refrigerating for at least 2 hours.
5. Top with whipped cream and serve chilled.

The Goose Girl's Honey-Cinnamon Biscotti

Ingredients:

- 1 1/2 cups all-purpose flour
- 1 tsp cinnamon
- 1/2 tsp baking powder
- 1/4 tsp salt
- 1/2 cup unsalted butter, softened
- 1/2 cup sugar
- 2 large eggs
- 1 tsp vanilla extract
- 1/4 cup honey
- 1/2 cup chopped almonds (optional)

Instructions:

1. Preheat the oven to 350°F (175°C). Line a baking sheet with parchment paper.
2. In a bowl, whisk together flour, cinnamon, baking powder, and salt.
3. In another bowl, cream together the butter and sugar until light and fluffy. Add eggs, one at a time, followed by vanilla extract and honey.
4. Gradually mix in the dry ingredients and stir in the almonds if using.
5. Shape the dough into a log and place on the prepared baking sheet. Bake for 25 minutes, or until golden.

6. Let the log cool for 10 minutes, then slice into 1-inch pieces.

7. Arrange the slices on the baking sheet and bake for an additional 10-15 minutes, until crisp.

The Little Prince's Asteroid Cake

Ingredients:

- 1 box chocolate cake mix (or homemade cake recipe)
- 1/2 cup powdered sugar
- 1/4 cup cocoa powder
- 1 cup heavy cream
- 1 tsp vanilla extract
- Sprinkles or edible stars for decoration

Instructions:

1. Prepare the chocolate cake according to the instructions on the box or using your favorite recipe.
2. Once the cake is baked and cooled, use a round cutter or your hands to form small asteroid-like shapes.
3. In a bowl, combine powdered sugar, cocoa powder, cream, and vanilla extract to make a smooth ganache.
4. Dip each asteroid cake into the ganache and place on a serving tray.
5. Decorate with sprinkles or edible stars to represent the magical stars of the Little Prince's world.

The Sorcerer's Stone's Dark Chocolate Truffles

Ingredients:

- 8 oz dark chocolate, chopped
- 1/2 cup heavy cream
- 1 tsp vanilla extract
- Cocoa powder or powdered sugar for dusting

Instructions:

1. Heat the heavy cream in a small saucepan until it begins to simmer. Pour over the chopped dark chocolate and let it sit for 1 minute.
2. Stir until the chocolate is fully melted and the mixture is smooth.
3. Add vanilla extract and let the ganache cool to room temperature.
4. Once cooled, use a spoon to scoop small amounts of ganache and roll them into balls.
5. Roll the truffles in cocoa powder or powdered sugar for a magical finish.
6. Refrigerate for at least 2 hours before serving.

Snow White's Snowflake Sugar Cookies

Ingredients:

- 2 1/2 cups all-purpose flour
- 1 tsp baking powder
- 1/4 tsp salt
- 1 cup unsalted butter, softened
- 1 cup granulated sugar
- 1 egg
- 1 tsp vanilla extract
- Powdered sugar for dusting

Instructions:

1. Preheat the oven to 350°F (175°C). Line a baking sheet with parchment paper.
2. In a bowl, whisk together the flour, baking powder, and salt.
3. In another bowl, cream the butter and sugar until light and fluffy. Add the egg and vanilla extract, mixing well.
4. Gradually add the dry ingredients to the butter mixture and mix until just combined.
5. Roll out the dough on a floured surface to about 1/4 inch thickness. Cut into snowflake shapes using a cookie cutter.
6. Place the cookies on the prepared baking sheet and bake for 8-10 minutes, or until the edges are lightly golden.
7. Let cool completely and dust with powdered sugar before serving.

www.ingramcontent.com/pod-product-compliance
Lightning Source LLC
LaVergne TN
LVHW081320060526
838201LV00055B/2389